SandCastle

Sound Words

Splish Splash

Kelly Doudna

Consulting Editor, Monica Marx, M.A./Reading Specialist

ABDO
Publishing Company

Published by SandCastle™, an imprint of ABDO Publishing Company, 4940 Viking Drive, Edina, Minnesota 55435.

Printed in the United States.

Credits
Edited by: Pam Price
Curriculum Coordinator: Nancy Tuminelly
Cover and Interior Design and Production: Mighty Media
Photo Credits: Corbis Images, Eyewire Images, Hemera, Image Source, PhotoDisc

Library of Congress Cataloging-in-Publication Data

Doudna, Kelly, 1963-
    Splish splash / Kelly Doudna.
        p. cm. -- (Sound words)
    "SandCastle books"--T.p. verso.
    Summary: Uses photographs and simple sentences to introduce words for noises related to weather that sound like what they describe, such as the whoosh of a gust of wind or the boom of thunder.
    ISBN 1-59197-453-4
    1. English language--Onomatopoeic words--Juvenile literature. 2. Sounds, Words for--Juvenile literature. [1. English language--Onomatopoeic words. 2. Sounds, Words for.] I. Title.

PE1597.D6357 2003
428.1--dc22
                                                                    2003048916

SandCastle™ books are created by a professional team of educators, reading specialists, and content developers around five essential components that include phonemic awareness, phonics, vocabulary, text comprehension, and fluency. All books are written, reviewed, and leveled for guided reading, early intervention reading, and Accelerated Reader® programs and designed for use in shared, guided, and independent reading and writing activities to support a balanced approach to literacy instruction.

Let Us Know

After reading the book, SandCastle would like you to tell us your stories about reading. What is your favorite page? Was there something hard that you needed help with? Share the ups and downs of learning to read. We want to hear from you! To get posted on the ABDO Publishing Company Web site, send us e-mail at:

sandcastle@abdopub.com

SandCastle Level: Transitional

Onomatopoeia
(on-uh-mat-uh-**pee**-uh)
is the use of words that
sound like what they
describe.

These **sound words** are
all around us.

swish swoosh!

bow wow!

tick tock!

splish splash!

clink clank!

tee hee!

3

Liz listens to the falling rain.

Drip!

Hope hears a gust of wind.

Whoosh!

Larry listens to the leaves flutter.

Swish!

Henry hears a clap of thunder.

Boom!

Lily looks at lightning.

Flash!

Ray runs through a puddle.

Splish splash!

Whoosh goes the wind
wheezing through the trees.

Swoosh go the leaves swishing
in the breeze.

Flash goes the lightning
bolting across the sky.

Crash bang is the thunder's reply.

Pitter patter goes the rain on the ground.

Splish splash go the drops all around.

Picture Index

drip, p. 5

flash, pp. 13, 18

pitter patter, p. 20

splish splash, pp. 15, 21

swish, p. 9

whoosh, pp. 7, 16

Glossary

breeze   a slow gentle wind

flutter   to flap or wave rapidly

gust   a sudden rush of wind

lightning a flash of light caused by electricity in the sky

thunder a loud sound that follows a flash of lightning

About SandCastle™

A professional team of educators, reading specialists, and content developers created the SandCastle™ series to support young readers as they develop reading skills and strategies and increase their general knowledge. The SandCastle™ series has four levels that correspond to early literacy development in young children. The levels are provided to help teachers and parents select the appropriate books for young readers.

Emerging Readers
(no flags)

Beginning Readers
(1 flag)

Transitional Readers
(2 flags)

Fluent Readers
(3 flags)

These levels are meant only as a guide. All levels are subject to change.

To see a complete list of SandCastle™ books and other nonfiction titles from ABDO Publishing Company, visit **www.abdopub.com** or contact us at:

4940 Viking Drive, Edina, Minnesota 55435 • 1-800-800-1312 • fax: 1-952-831-1632